MW01178489

TSUNAMI READINESS

Simon Rose

Crabtree Publishing Company
www.crabtreebooks.com

CRABTREE
PUBLISHING COMPANY
WWW.CRABTREEBOOKS.COM

Author: Simon Rose

Series research and development:
Janine Deschenes, Reagan Miller

Editorial director: Kathy Middleton

Editors: Ellen Rodger, Melissa Boyce

Proofreader: Wendy Scavuzzo

Design and photo research:
Katherine Berti

Prepress technician:
Tammy McGarr

Print and production coordinator:
Katherine Berti

Images:

Alamy Stock Photo
dpa picture alliance archive: p. 28
North Wind Picture Archives: p. 5
Science History Images: p. 30, 31 (top)
Flickr: Kevin Gill: p. 35 (top)
NASA:JPL-Caltech: p. 38
NOAA: p. 19 (both insets bottom left), 23 (both)
Teacher at Sea Program: front cover (bottom)
podaac.jpl.nasa.gov: Screen Shot 2019-08-26 at 4.19.53 PM: p. 39 (laptop inset)
Sadatsugu Tomizawa, Jiji Press: p. 13
Shutterstock
BNK Maritime Photographer: p. 17 (center)
C and L Perry: p. 41
Casper1774 Studio: p. 6–7
Frans Delian: p. 14, 25
KenSoftTH: p. 9
Marc van Vuren: p. 26 (top)
Smallcreative: p. 8
Terry Kelly: p. 46
testing: p. 35 (center)
Wikimedia Commons
四葉亭四迷: p. 40
Aretitea Teeta, AusAID, Department of Foreign Affairs and Trade: p. 36 (bottom)
Batholith: p. 18 (bottom)
CEphoto, Uwe Aranas: p. 42
David Rydevik (email david.rydevik@gmail.com) Stockholm, Sweden: p. 1, 26 (bottom)
Sed: p. 32
United States Geological Survey, Photo courtesy of the Pacific Tsunami Museum in Hilo, Hawai`i: p. 22
U.S. Air Force: Tech. Sgt. Cohen A. Young: p. 29 (top)
USARJ NCO CORPS: p. 27
U.S. Marine Corps: Lance Cpl. Hugh S. Holder III: p. 43
U.S. Navy
Mass Communication Specialist 3rd Class Alexander Tidd: p. 33
Mass Communication Specialist 3rd Class Dylan McCord: p. 20, 21
Photographer's Mate 2nd Class Katrina Beeler: p. 14 (center left)
Photographer's Mate 2nd Class Philip A. McDaniel: p. 15 (top left)
Photographer's Mate 3rd Class Gabriel R. Piper: p. 15 (right)
Van.takacs: p. 24
All other images by Shutterstock

Library and Archives Canada Cataloguing in Publication

Title: Tsunami readiness / Simon Rose.
Names: Rose, Simon, 1961- author.
Description: Series statement: Natural disasters: meeting the challenge | Includes bibliographical references and index.
Identifiers: Canadiana (print) 20190134372 | Canadiana (ebook) 20190134380 | ISBN 9780778765240 (hardcover) | ISBN 9780778765301 (softcover) | ISBN 9781427123824 (HTML)
Subjects: LCSH: Tsunamis—Juvenile literature. | LCSH: Emergency management—Juvenile literature.
Classification: LCC GC221.5 .R67 2019 | DDC j551.46/37—dc23

Library of Congress Cataloging-in-Publication Data

Names: Rose, Simon, 1961- author.
Title: Tsunami readiness / Simon Rose.
Description: New York : Crabtree Publishing Company, 2019. | Series: Natural disasters: meeting the challenge | Includes bibliographical references and index.
Identifiers: LCCN 2019025174 (print) | LCCN 2019025175 (ebook) | ISBN 9780778765240 (hardcover) | ISBN 9780778765301 (paperback) | ISBN 9781427123824 (ebook)
Subjects: LCSH: Tsunamis--Juvenile literature. | Tsunami hazard zones--Juvenile literature. | Emergency management--Juvenile literature. | Natural disasters--Juvenile literature.
Classification: LCC GC221.5 .R67 2019 (print) | LCC GC221.5 (ebook) | DDC 363.34/94--dc23
LC record available at https://lccn.loc.gov/2019025174
LC ebook record available at https://lccn.loc.gov/2019025175

Crabtree Publishing Company

www.crabtreebooks.com   1-800-387-7650

Printed in the U.S.A./102019/CG20190809

Published in Canada
Crabtree Publishing
616 Welland Ave.
St. Catharines, Ontario
L2M 5V6

Published in the United States
Crabtree Publishing
PMB 59051
350 Fifth Avenue, 59th Floor
New York, New York 10118

Published in the United Kingdom
Crabtree Publishing
Maritime House
Basin Road North, Hove
BN41 1WR

Published in Australia
Crabtree Publishing
Unit 3–5 Currumbin Court
Capalaba
QLD 4157

Contents

What Is a Tsunami?

Tsunami is a Japanese word that means "harbor wave." A tsunami is made up of large ocean waves created by a sudden and large-scale disturbance of the seawater. Tsunamis are mostly caused by **earthquakes** or **volcanic eruptions**. They can also be caused by undersea **landslides** or by **meteors** hitting Earth.

Ring of Fire

Eighty percent of tsunamis occur in the Pacific Ocean where there are many underwater earthquakes and volcanoes. The area around the Pacific where more than 75 percent of the world's volcanoes are located is called the Ring of Fire.

Countries bordering the Pacific Ocean Ring of Fire, such as the United States, Canada, Chile, and Japan, are most at risk from tsunamis. However, tsunamis also happen in other parts of the world. A 2004 tsunami in the Indian Ocean killed more than 230,000 people.

Warning Systems

Many coastal areas have tsunami warning systems that alert people, allowing them time to evacuate the area. The warning system in the Pacific Ocean is called the DART system. This stands for Deep-ocean Assessment and Reporting of Tsunamis.

Major tsunamis in the last 100 years:

Year	Location	Deaths
1908	MESSINA, ITALY	123,000
2011	TOHOKU, JAPAN	18,500
1960	VALDIVIA, CHILE, PACIFIC OCEAN	6,000
2004	INDIAN OCEAN	230,210
1976	MORO GULF, PHILIPPINES	5,000

Devastating Waves

Throughout history, tsunamis have caused enormous damage and killed millions of people. Around 1500 B.C.E., a volcanic eruption devastated the Greek island of Thera, now called Santorini. The eruption's tremors touched off a tsunami that swept the island of Crete. The devastating wave caused the collapse of the ancient **Minoan civilization** on the island. The disaster might have inspired the legend of **Atlantis**, a fictional story of an island swallowed by the ocean after a series of earthquakes.

The most powerful earthquake in recorded history struck southern Chile in 1960. The quake caused tsunamis with waves up to 82 feet (25 m) high in Chile. The main tsunami traveled across the Pacific Ocean, causing deaths, injuries, and damage as far away as Japan, the Philippines, and New Zealand. The town of Hilo in Hawaii was also hit by the tsunami, causing 61 deaths.

An illustration of the earthquake and tsunami that hit Lisbon, Portugal, in 1755. Lisbon was almost completely destroyed as a result of the natural disaster.

Hazards and Disasters

Tsunamis are natural hazards that can become disasters when communities do not have the ability to prepare for or recover from them.

Scale of Disasters

Natural disasters are defined in terms of the number of people affected and the damage caused to buildings and important **infrastructure**. The scale of a disaster also depends on what kinds of challenges there are to helping people recover, rebuild, and repair damages. These things are known as the relief effort. Sometimes, geography is a problem. If the tsunami occurs in a remote area or one that's hard to reach, such as an isolated group of islands, it may take more time for help and materials to arrive. A disaster is also defined by the possibility of something similar happening again, and how people in the area have learned to **adapt** after previous incidents. Where people live has a lot to do with how vulnerable they are to disaster.

Scientists study tsunamis to learn more about their effects. Technology is also available to monitor and try to predict tsunamis. This helps us to be ready for them and to minimize the scale of damage and the number of deaths and injuries.

*A tsunami **evacuation** building in Thailand*

อาคารหลบภัย
TSUNAMI

Being prepared for disasters includes having safety systems in place for protecting buildings and infrastructure, as well as for evacuations, shelters, food and water, and medical supplies. Tsunami experts recommend people know their communities and all the possible routes out of them. They suggest practicing walking evacuation routes—including in darkness.

TSUNAMI
EVACUATION
ROUTE

CASE STUDY
The Tohoku Earthquake and Tsunami of 2011

On March 11, 2011, Japan was hit by the most powerful earthquake ever recorded in the country. Called the Great East Japan Earthquake, it caused a tsunami with waves up to 132 feet (40 m) high. More than 15,800 people were killed and another 450,000 people were left homeless. A further 3,084 were declared missing. Many areas of the country were flooded. Some waves went inland as far as 6.2 miles (10 km), carrying buildings and cars with them.

The tsunami also damaged the Fukushima **nuclear plant**, releasing **radiation**. There were also fires and explosions at the plant. More than 200,000 people were evacuated from the area surrounding the nuclear plant. Sewage treatment plants, fish processing plants, and city services were damaged or destroyed.

The 2011 earthquake and tsunami in Japan destroyed

138,000 BUILDINGS and caused
$360 BILLION in damages.

In Japan, around **245 MILES (394 KM)** of seawalls have been built. Some of those built since the 2011 tsunami are more than **40 FEET (12 M) HIGH.**

Since the disaster, Japan has updated its tsunami mitigation plan, taking into account evacuation plans for future disasters and creating new tsunami warning and protection systems. The aim was to rebuild cities and towns to make them more earthquake and tsunami resistant. In Kushimoto, residents were moved to areas of higher elevation where there was less risk of flooding. Earth and sand was used to build up lowland areas and seawalls in several cities. Building construction was restricted in low-lying areas. In some cities, police, fire, and rescue buildings were moved to higher locations inland. This was done to ensure these services would be able to respond during future tsunamis.

This floodgate in Numazu, Japan, was built to protect the city from tsunamis caused by earthquakes. In the event of a strong earthquake, the gate will automatically close.

CHAPTER 1

The Science Behind Tsunamis

Earth Movements

Tsunamis are giant waves that have several causes, including underwater earthquakes, volcanoes, landslides, and even meteorites that hit oceans. Earthquakes are the most common cause. They happen when large pieces of Earth's crust, called tectonic plates, bump and slide into each other. The edges of the plates are called plate boundaries. These have many faults, or large cracks, and most earthquakes occur there.

Tsunamis can also happen where there are underwater volcanoes. These types of earthquakes are caused by fault lines or by magma moving inside the volcano.

Russia

Japan

United States

RING OF FIRE

Australia

Pacific Ocean

The Ring of Fire around the Pacific Ocean is very prone to volcanic and earthquake activity. In this area, many of the planet's tectonic plates border each other. This is why tsunamis are most common in the Pacific.

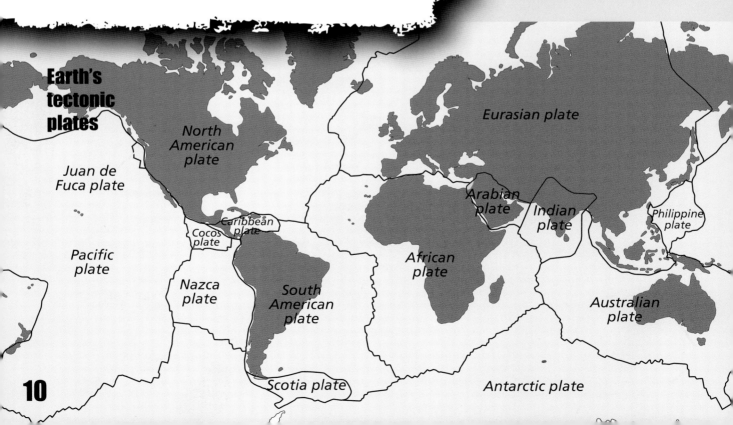

Earth's tectonic plates

Juan de Fuca plate

North American plate

Eurasian plate

Arabian plate

Indian plate

Philippine plate

Caribbean plate

Cocos plate

Pacific plate

African plate

Nazca plate

South American plate

Australian plate

Scotia plate

Antarctic plate

Moving Fast

Tsunamis quickly travel thousands of miles across the ocean. A normal ocean wave driven by wind travels at around 55.9 miles per hour (90 kph). Tsunami waves can travel at speeds of about 500 miles per hour (805 kph) or more. This is almost the same speed as a jet airplane.

How High?

In deep water, tsunami waves are less than 3 feet (1 m) high. This means that tsunamis can be difficult to detect when they are still a long way from the coastline. People on ships far out at sea might not even notice a tsunami wave passing underneath them as it is so small. Tsunamis slow down as they approach shallow water near the coast. However, they might still be moving at more than 50 miles per hour (80 kph). When a tsunami hits the shore, the first wave might not be the biggest. Very often, bigger and stronger waves arrive later.

Tsunamis don't look like normal wind-generated waves that break as they come ashore. Instead, tsunami waves come onshore as a rapidly rising surge of water.

Big Tub of Water

Part of the ocean floor is raised or dropped as a result of an underwater earthquake or volcanic eruption. This causes the water to rise and spread, or become **displaced**. This is similar to a person moving in a full bathtub. If the person moves forward, waves are created. Imagine this happening in the ocean with a huge amount of water. Waves spread outward like ripples do when a pebble is thrown into water. The ripples then form wider and wider circles as they spread outward.

The Trough

The first sign of the arrival of a tsunami at the coast is often called the trough of the wave. This means that the water draws back and exposes the seafloor near the shoreline. Fish and other marine animals can be seen on the newly exposed ground. People sometimes walk into this open area to help animals or people or to collect their belongings. This can be very dangerous as the main part of the tsunami is still on its way.

First Wave

The first huge wave arrives a few minutes after the water has drawn back. Tsunami waves get bigger as they get closer to the shore. The waves can be more than 100 feet (30.5 m) high when they reach the coastline. The level of the seawater can increase to great heights in as little as 10 to 15 minutes. Waves might continue to arrive for several hours after the first one hits the coast.

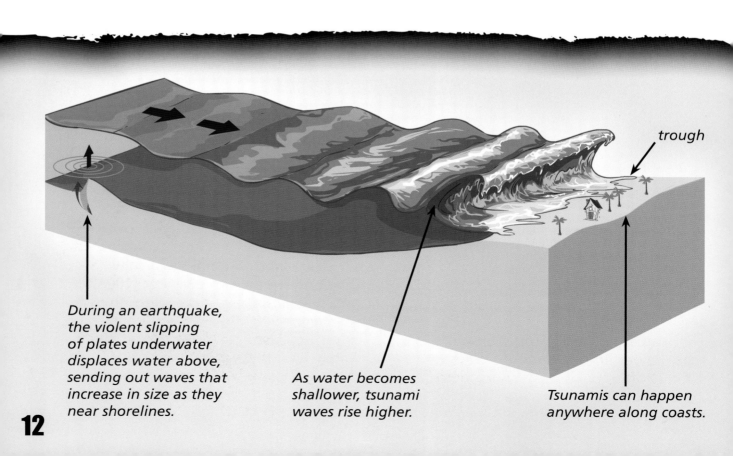

trough

During an earthquake, the violent slipping of plates underwater displaces water above, sending out waves that increase in size as they near shorelines.

As water becomes shallower, tsunami waves rise higher.

Tsunamis can happen anywhere along coasts.

Large tsunamis can cause damage to coastal areas thousands of miles away from the earthquake that caused them.

BAYS, LAGOONS, and HARBORS *can increase the effects of a tsunami by funneling water rapidly into inland areas.*

Wall of Water

A fast-moving, powerful, high wall of water will cause a lot of damage. Large tsunami waves destroy low-lying areas and towns and cities on the coast. They also travel a long way inland. The furious rush of water is very forceful. It moves large boats, cars, power lines, and debris inland. **Debris** often crashes into buildings as the power of the wave and flooding waters washes everything inland.

Wavelength

The wavelength, or the distance between each wave, determines how far a tsunami can travel inland. A normal storm will have a wavelength of about 328 feet (100 m). A tsunami might have a wavelength of up to 310 miles (500 km). The geography along the coastline also affects how far the water moves inland. If the coastline is mostly flat, with no cliffs or mountains, the waves will go farther. This means tsunamis in different parts of the world are not always the same.

CASE STUDY
The Indian Ocean Tsunami of 2004

The Indian Ocean tsunami occurred on December 26, 2004. The underwater earthquake that triggered the massive tsunami was one of the largest ever recorded, with a **magnitude** of 9.0. The epicenter, or where the earthquake is felt the strongest, was near the west coast of the island of Sumatra in Indonesia, but the tsunamis it created hit Indonesia, Thailand, Sri Lanka, India, Malaysia, and several other countries. The earthquake created tsunamis up to 100 feet high (30 m) that quickly moved across the Indian Ocean.

India Myanmar

Indian Ocean

Thailand

Sri Lanka earthquake epicenter Malaysia

Indonesia

Legend

● *Worst-affected areas*

In 2012, the warning system notified people of an earthquake in Banda Aceh, Indonesia, where some of the worst damage occurred in the 2004 tsunami.

Following the 2004 Indian Ocean tsunami, the U.S. Navy delivered emergency food and other supplies, and provided medical treatment to those affected.

Death Toll

More than 200,000 people were killed in countries bordering the Indian Ocean. In Indonesia alone, 130,736 people were confirmed dead. Several hours lapsed between the earthquake and when the tsunamis reached land, but people were taken by surprise. There was no warning system. Towns, villages, farmland, and fishing grounds were destroyed. Salt water also damaged and destroyed crops in the areas affected, making recovery difficult as people who survived also lost their ability to feed themselves and make a living.

Relief, Recovery, Rebuilding

Roads were damaged in remote areas, making relief and recovery efforts difficult in some of the areas hit. At first, there was a lack of food, clean water, and medical supplies. Billions of dollars of aid poured in from countries all over the world and relief efforts concentrated on preventing disease outbreaks. Over time, the areas were rebuilt. The disaster prompted a change in safety warnings. The Indian Ocean Tsunami Warning System was set up in 2005. It consists of 25 seismographic relaying stations where information on potential tsunamis is passed on to 26 national centers. When an earthquake takes place and a tsunami is likely, tsunami warning **sirens** go off and people are directed to evacuate.

CHAPTER 2

Studying Disasters and Their Effects

Tsunamis are a natural hazard that are studied by several different kinds of scientists. Some look at how different types of tsunamis are caused, while others examine their effects. Still others look at the history of tsunamis. All help to gather knowledge on how these killer waves can be mitigated, or made less of a severe threat to human lives and livelihoods.

What They Do

Seismology is the study of things caused by or related to earthquakes. Seismologists are scientists that study **seismic** waves. Earthquakes are caused by seismic waves passing through Earth's rocks. These waves are produced when energy stored in the planet's crust is suddenly released. The waves travel through rock up to ground level on land or under the sea and cause damage on Earth's surface.

It isn't possible to accurately predict when a tsunami will happen, but we can study previous tsunamis and watch areas prone to earthquakes or where there are volcanoes.

Geologists

Geologists study Earth, the materials it is made of, and the processes that affect them. They also look at how these things have changed over time. Geologists work to understand natural events such as earthquakes, landslides, floods, and volcanic eruptions. They can then advise where people, buildings, and infrastructure might be at risk from natural disasters. They also use data, or information from the past to study **climate change** and what this might mean in the future.

Volcano and Ocean Experts

Volcanologists are geologists that specialize in the study of volcanoes. Their work involves how volcanoes are formed, the processes in volcanic eruptions, and the study of previous eruptions. Oceanographers study many things related to the planet's oceans and coastal waters, including underwater geology and the shifting of tectonic plates under the sea. Hydrologists study the water on the surface, underground, and in the atmosphere of our planet.

A research ship places tsunami detection **buoys** into the waters around Thailand.

Scientists estimate about 100 tsunamis occur each year in the Great Lakes. Most are small meteotsunamis, or meteorological tsunamis of a few inches high, but some can reach more than 6 feet (2 m).

CASE STUDY
Underwater Trench Research

Scientists study the processes that lead to tsunamis to understand what might happen during future tsunamis. Research done on the 2011 Great East Japan earthquake and tsunami will likely help forecasters for decades to come. The tsunami was caused when a shallow area close to the Japan Trench slipped 164–280 feet (50–85 m) and raised the seabed. Before this, researchers had thought shallow areas did not experience earthquake-causing slips.

Researchers took a deep-sea scientific drilling vessel down 22,637 feet (6,900 m) underwater. It drilled boreholes in the ocean floor in the fault zone. Known as the Japan Trench Fast Drilling Project, the researchers also studied water pressure, the **composition** of the seafloor rock, and how heat affected the water. Friction between the plates created temperatures of 932 degrees Fahrenheit (500 °C). This caused water trapped underneath to expand, pushing the fault open and leading to a large slip.

The information gained from this project will help scientists predict the chances of a large earthquake. It may even help determine its intensity, which will aid in forecasting the size of tsunamis.

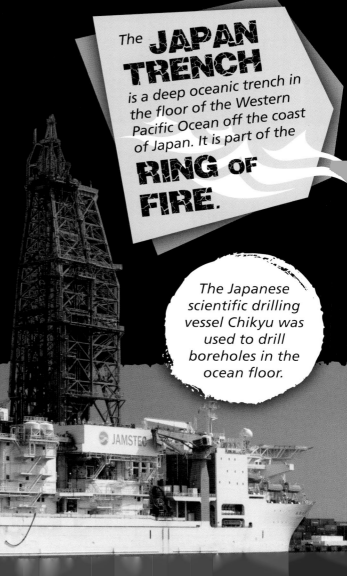

The **JAPAN TRENCH** is a deep oceanic trench in the floor of the Western Pacific Ocean off the coast of Japan. It is part of the **RING OF FIRE**.

The Japanese scientific drilling vessel Chikyu was used to drill boreholes in the ocean floor.

JAMSTEC

20

High-Tech Examinations

Scientists also monitor possible tsunamis with high-tech equipment including tide gauges that measure the height of the sea's surface and tide levels. The gauges have **sensors** that can detect changes in sea level that might mean a tsunami is coming. Devices called altimeters in **satellites** measure the height of the ocean surface using **electromagnetic** pulses. The DART system has monitoring stations in the Pacific Ocean. These also provide important information about tsunamis.

Modeling Tsunamis

Tsunami modeling research is conducted by the NOAA Center for Tsunami Research (NCTR) in the United States. Modeling is designed to simulate what might happen in a real situation. Numerical models are designed to provide more reliable and faster forecasts of tsunamis. The NCTR provides data, or information, that helps the world's tsunami warning centers forecast potential disasters.

Information to create the tsunami model is taken from sensors in the ocean and from satellites. This information is combined with the shape of the seafloor where seismic activity was detected, and details of nearby coastlines. Models are used to estimate the size and height of the waves, and when and where they might hit shore.

19

The large amount of water that a tsunami pushes ashore is called **the RUN-UP.** *Run-ups are damaging as they surge inland.*

Impact of Tsunamis

Tsunamis have a big impact both on the coastline and farther inland, depending on the size and strength of the event. Just about anything in the path of a tsunami on the land can be affected. This includes cars, boats, trees, and telephone and utility lines. Ships can be pushed inland and vehicles can be washed away. Homes, commercial buildings, and infrastructure can be damaged or destroyed. Buildings not constructed to withstand earthquakes and tsunamis collapse more easily. Fires are likely to break out because of broken gas lines, or from fallen electrical cables.

Escape Routes

People using vehicles to escape tsunamis are often caught in traffic jams. They might also be on roads that are blocked by debris caused by the tsunami. This means that they are very likely to be swept away if caught in a huge wave. The best way to escape is usually on foot. People need to get to higher ground such as slopes and hills as quickly as they can to stay away from the coming flood. If caught in the water, it is best to try to hang onto something that floats. It is better to just go with the **current** rather than try to swim.

Spread of Disease

After a tsunami, there is also the potential for the spread of disease from unrecovered bodies or if the local water supply is **contaminated**. Seawater from the tsunami can travel a long way inland. This can poison the soil and freshwater supplies with salt. This can lead to food shortages in the weeks after the tsunami. A lack of fresh water can also lead to deaths long after the disaster.

SCIENCE BIO
Hazard Research Centre

The Benfield UCL Hazard Research Centre was set up at University College London (UCL), United Kingdom, in 2006. It is one of Europe's leading centers for research and education on natural hazards and risks. UCL's EPICentre, founded a year later, focuses on risk reduction, with a major aim being reducing the loss of life and livelihoods through natural disasters.

EPICentre research projects include field missions that send scientists to areas affected by tsunamis to help determine how science can help reduce the impact of these natural hazards. The Hazard Research Centre collaborates with the EPICentre to share the work done by scientists on natural disasters, and makes it useful to people, businesses, and governments. Examples of the work include a paper on successful early warning systems for disasters,

a conference on risk reduction, and training for people who work in the insurance industry.

The Hazard Research Centre operates programs that help reduce the risk to people's lives and property during natural disasters, as well as improving emergency response and relief. The center also does modeling of "mega-thrust" earthquakes and the tsunamis resulting from them. Through a program called CRUST (Cascading Risk and Uncertainty assessment of earthquake Shaking and Tsunami), the powerful waves are **simulated** on computer so experts can examine how bad the destruction and flooding would be in a specific town or city. The information is then used to develop better building construction materials and methods, as well as better rescue and relief practices.

Members of the Japanese military and disaster relief crews search for victims of a 9.0-magnitude earthquake and subsequent tsunami in Sukuiso, Japan, in 2011.

CHAPTER 3

Meeting the Challenge

Set up in 1949 after a devastating earthquake and tsunami, the Pacific Tsunami Warning Center (PTWC) has become a lifesaving network for people living on the west coast of North America. The 1946 Aleutian Islands earthquake and tsunami in the North Pacific caused a deadly tsunami in Alaska and Hawaii. The tsunami wiped out the Scotch Cap Lighthouse on Alaska's Unimak Island. This prevented warnings being sent to Hawaii. Almost five hours later, giant waves hit Hilo, Hawaii, killing 173 people and destroying almost 500 buildings. Up and running three years after the Hilo disaster, the PTWC monitors seismic activity in the Pacific Ocean. It is operated by the National Oceanic and Atmospheric Administration (NOAA), and is based in Hawaii.

National Tsunami Warning Center

The NOAA also operates the National Tsunami Warning Center (NTWC) based in Alaska. The NTWC was established in 1967 to provide tsunami warnings for regions on North America's west coast, such as Alaska, British Columbia, Washington, Oregon, and California. All the countries that have coastlines on the Pacific are connected to the PTWC.

The tsunami traveled at about **500 MILES PER HOUR** (805 kph), with waves of more than **55 FEET** (17 m).

People in Hilo run from an approaching wave during the 1946 tsunami. Hilo's location on a funnel-shaped bay makes it more vulnerable to tsunami waves. A 1960 tsunami claimed 60 lives in Hilo, but that time, experts say the deaths were mainly caused by people ignoring warning sirens.

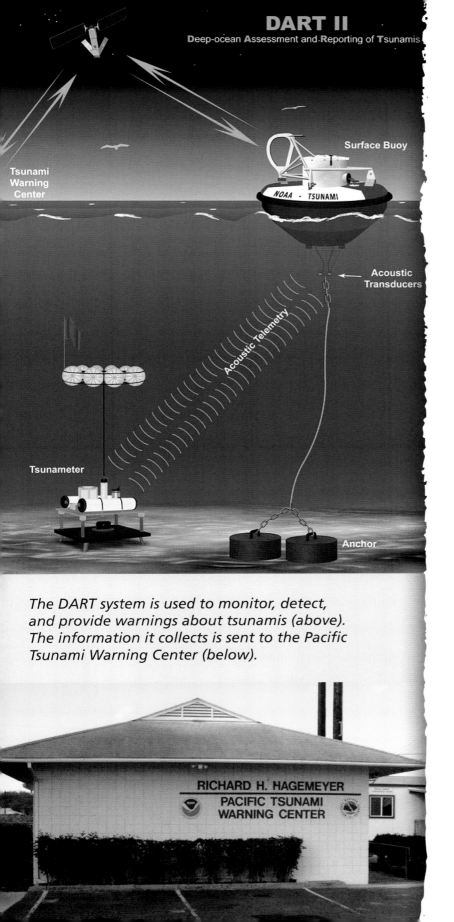

Surface Buoy

Tsunami Warning Center

NOAA - TSUNAMI

Acoustic Transducers

Acoustic Telemetry

Tsunameter

Anchor

The DART system is used to monitor, detect, and provide warnings about tsunamis (above). The information it collects is sent to the Pacific Tsunami Warning Center (below).

RICHARD H. HAGEMEYER
PACIFIC TSUNAMI
WARNING CENTER

Tsunami Detectives

Detecting tsunamis early is key to saving lives. Given enough warning, people can follow safety drills and evacuation routes to higher ground. The DART system is used to monitor, detect, and provide warnings about tsunamis. DART stations are placed in areas of the Pacific that have a history of tsunamis. Each station has a surface buoy and seafloor bottom pressure recording (BPR) equipment. The bottom pressure recorders and the surface buoys are replaced regularly to make sure that they are always working.

Satellite Warning

When the BPR detects a tsunami, the information is sent to the buoy by **sonar**. The buoy then sends the information via satellite to the PTWC. As the tsunami wave moves across the ocean and passes other buoys and BPRs, more data is sent. This provides a better picture of the tsunami's direction, strength, size, and where it might hit land. The DART system has been very useful for issuing tsunami warnings and allowing people to prepare to evacuate an area that is at risk.

23

CASE STUDY
The Indian Ocean Tsunami Warning System

The Indian Ocean Tsunami Warning System was developed after the 2004 Indian Ocean earthquake. The tsunami that followed that earthquake left 230,000 people dead or missing. The devastation and enormous loss of life prompted several countries to agree, at a **United Nations** meeting, to setting up an international early warning system. The Indian Ocean Tsunami Warning System provides advance notification of tsunamis to the countries bordering the ocean in East Africa, India, Burma, Thailand, Indonesia, Australia, and others. The system became operational in June 2006.

Seismographic Stations

The system's 25 seismographic stations send information to 26 national tsunami information centers. They also send data to six DART buoys that are stationed far out at sea. A pressure recorder on the seabed measures the weight of the water above it. The weight varies depending on the height of the waves, and a buoy sends the data and information on surface conditions to a satellite in orbit around Earth. The satellite then forwards the details to a receiving station on the ground. Because the DART system detects tsunamis far out at sea, it is able to provide plenty of warning time.

A pressure recorder and tsunami waves detector being submerged in the ocean. Technology such as this provides advance notification of tsunamis, giving people more time to evacuate.

A ship pushed by the 2004 tsunami landed on the roofs of houses in Banda Aceh, Indonesia.

GLOSS

The Global Sea Level Observing System (GLOSS) uses tide gauges on mainland coasts or on islands out at sea. Basic gauges monitor the surface of the water with a system of tubes and floats. Others "ping" the surface from above with **radar** or sonar. Some gauges also use seabed pressure sensors that are connected by a cable to a station that monitors the sea level. There are around 70 GLOSS stations in the Indian Ocean. These send data by satellite to national tsunami centers

Sending Out Warnings

Information from the system is processed at the Pacific Tsunami Warning Center in Hawaii. Data from the Indian Ocean is also processed by the Japan Meteorological Agency. Areas that are threatened by a tsunami are alerted. They then warn people living in the areas of the danger. Warnings can be sent by television, radio, online, or via mobile phones. Some countries also have warning sirens along the coastline that sound when a tsunami is about to arrive

Emergency Alerts

People living in areas at risk of tsunamis are warned about them in a number of ways. In the United States, warnings are sent to the National Weather Service. They are also sent to local government and emergency officials. Emergency alert systems send messages to all TV and radio stations. Messages are also sent to businesses, homes, hospitals, and schools. In the state of Washington, outdoor siren systems alert people in more remote areas.

Educating About Tsunamis

Education about alerts is very important, as well. People living in coastal areas are at risk during a tsunami. Many communities have taken tsunamis into account when approving new buildings—ensuring that they are built away from coastal shores and on higher ground. In 2015–2016, the U.S. House of Representatives passed the Tsunami Warning, Education, and Research Act that improves tsunami warning system forecasts for arrival, as well as damage estimates. The bill established working groups to provide advice on tsunami science and technology. It also supports community outreach programs that encourage people to take warnings seriously.

If people ignore warnings and sirens and don't follow directions to head to higher ground, they risk their lives.

Most tsunami waves are less than **10 FEET (3 M) HIGH,** *but they can be greater than* **100 FEET (30 M) HIGH.**

In Japan, tsunami preparation is a mandatory requirement for all levels of government, as well as for local emergency service providers. The U.S. Army has participated in annual disaster training exercises in Japan since 2010.

Issuing Warnings

If the DART stations report a tsunami that might cause a large impact on the coastline, a tsunami warning is issued. This is for areas that are expected to be hit within an hour. Local officials will tell people about the coming danger and order the evacuation of coastal areas at risk. The local population will be warned about the possibility of floods. People are also informed that powerful waves might continue for a while after the first waves hit the shore. Warnings might later be updated, downgraded, or canceled, based on new information about the tsunami from the warning system.

Advisories and Watches

A tsunami advisory is different from a warning. An advisory is issued when there is a tsunami that might produce waves dangerous to those near or in the water. The advisory is issued when the tsunami is expected to arrive or is already happening. Emergency services might decide to evacuate harbors and close beaches. An advisory might be updated to a warning or canceled, based on data from the warning system. Different from an advisory, a tsunami watch is issued when a tsunami might later hit the watch area. A watch may be upgraded to a warning or an advisory based on information from the warning system. It may also be canceled once the danger has passed.

Search and Rescue

Following a tsunami, emergency services and search-and-rescue workers quickly try to help as many people as possible. Emergency rescue and medical help are the first things that are needed. They are usually the first on the scene as well. In some areas, military personnel and local police forces are also involved in the rescue operation. Areas of the world that are unable to cope with the devastation of a tsunami often rely on international aid organizations. These include United Nations agencies, the **Red Cross**, and **Doctors Without Borders**.

Destroyed Infrastructure

Tsunamis damage or destroy low-lying infrastructure such as bridges, roads, and hospitals. As the wall of water comes inland, it picks up mud, rubble from buildings, vehicles, and other debris. Survivors have no way to escape the rushing water except to get above it by climbing trees, rushing up hills, or finding shelter in tall buildings—if the buildings are stable. That's why rescue services use helicopters to get survivors off of roofs. With infrastructure destroyed, communities have a difficult time maintaining services. No roads, hospitals, or water and sewage treatment plants mean people's basic needs can't be met. Relief efforts have to meet basic requirements of medical care, food, and clean water first, before housing and longer-term needs can be met.

New research suggests a **1607** wave that caused **2,000 DEATHS** in the Bristol Channel, U.K., was likely a tsunami caused by an earthquake in the seafloor near southwest Ireland.

The largest single rail disaster happened in 2004 during the Indian Ocean earthquake. A tsunami swamped a passenger train in Sri Lanka, killing more than 1,700 people.

Pinned by Rubble

People are often buried in rubble from fallen buildings or other structures after a tsunami. Many are killed when they are hit by floating debris or pushed violently into buildings or other standing objects. Some survive being tossed about, but are injured. Rescue workers use different ways to try to find these survivors. Small video cameras on the ends of long poles are slipped into gaps in the rubble to search for people. **Thermal imaging** equipment is used to detect warm bodies. Special sound equipment can listen for any sounds that might come from people still alive under the rubble. If people are still breathing underground, detectors are used to locate the **carbon dioxide** that they are breathing out. Rescue workers use these types of equipment so that rubble is quickly removed in the right place to reach the injured.

Fallen live electrical cables or broken gas lines can create hazards. They might also cause fires to break out.

Rescue and cadaver dogs have a very strong sense of smell. These dogs are used to search for victims in the rubble. The dogs can find people that humans can't easily locate.

After the Tsunami

Most of the damage caused by a tsunami happens after the first powerful wave. The run-up is rising water that follows and floods the area while also pushing debris and weakening structures. Broken bones, cuts, and injuries from being crushed are common in people who survive a run-up.

The dirty aftermath of a tsunami, where dead bodies, debris, and dirty water from broken sewer pipes combine to cause disease, is a serious threat to the lives of survivors. Rescue workers stress the importance of communities having clean water after a disaster. This can help prevent the spread of diseases such as **cholera** and **dysentery,** as well as skin infections. Relief agencies often gather people together in temporary camps to provide care. It's easier to feed, shelter, and treat people when they are assembled in one central area.

An aerial view of Sumatra, Indonesia, before the Indian Ocean earthquake and tsunami of 2004

Recovery

Long-term recovery from a tsunami begins after the search-and-rescue efforts are over. It's likely that most infrastructure, such as government buildings, hospitals, and schools, needs to be repaired or rebuilt. Local governments might also need help from outside to rebuild. International relief organizations, private companies, and local people work together to get things done. If the tsunami struck in a remote area, there will often be major challenges in getting help where it is needed.

Planning for the Future

Part of the recovery effort is planning for the future. This will help an area to cope more easily in the event of another tsunami. Preparedness is a part of tsunami resilience. It includes building structures that mitigate, or lessen, the dangers of these powerful waves because damages caused by tsunamis can lead to disasters.

Building for Tsunamis

One way of lessening danger is to improve the building codes in earthquake- and tsunami-prone regions. Building codes are rules that set out the standards for constructing buildings. They are established by governments. The codes may include things such as using materials that lessen the risk of fire, or ensuring that building foundations are made from strong material. Seismic codes are building codes made specifically to protect property from earthquakes. Some building codes include tsunami protection.

In the United States, there are no national standards of engineering and design for tsunami protection, but the American Society of Civil Engineers has a guideline for tsunami-resilient design. It suggests using "inundation maps" in tsunami-prone areas. These are maps that show low-lying coastal areas that are likely to be swamped and flooded during a tsunami. It is recommended that buildings be located away from these areas.

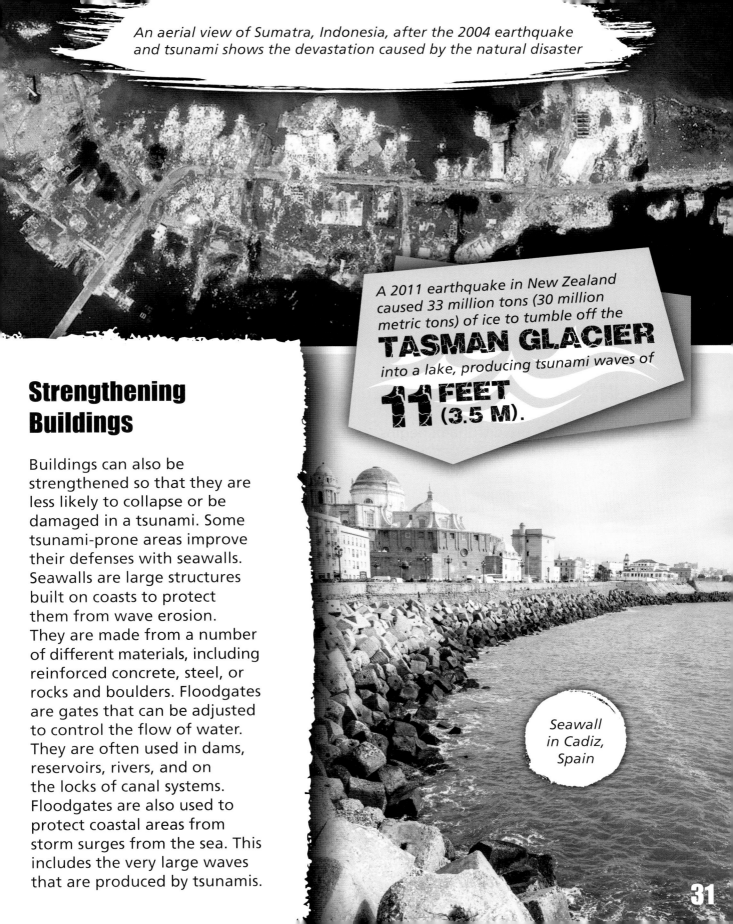

An aerial view of Sumatra, Indonesia, after the 2004 earthquake and tsunami shows the devastation caused by the natural disaster

A 2011 earthquake in New Zealand caused 33 million tons (30 million metric tons) of ice to tumble off the **TASMAN GLACIER** into a lake, producing tsunami waves of **11 FEET (3.5 M).**

Strengthening Buildings

Buildings can also be strengthened so that they are less likely to collapse or be damaged in a tsunami. Some tsunami-prone areas improve their defenses with seawalls. Seawalls are large structures built on coasts to protect them from wave erosion. They are made from a number of different materials, including reinforced concrete, steel, or rocks and boulders. Floodgates are gates that can be adjusted to control the flow of water. They are often used in dams, reservoirs, rivers, and on the locks of canal systems. Floodgates are also used to protect coastal areas from storm surges from the sea. This includes the very large waves that are produced by tsunamis.

Seawall in Cadiz, Spain

CASE STUDY
Fudai Floodgate

Fudai is a village in northeastern Japan. In 1933, a tsunami killed more than 400 people in the area. Between 1972 and 1984, a floodgate was built to protect the village. It is 51 feet (15.5 m) high and 673 feet (205 m) wide. Most local residents didn't like the structure at first, and many people thought that building it was a waste of public money. But it proved its worth in 2011, when the village was protected from damage during the 2011 Tohoku earthquake and tsunami. Some of the tsunami waves were more than 60 feet (18 m) high. They eventually crashed over and broke the floodgate, but the barrier did protect the village from the main force of the waves. Instead of a death toll in the hundreds, Fudai reported one person missing after the disaster. A lower, 30-foot (9 m) seawall in a nearby town of Otsuchi was completely destroyed. Japan is now constructing a 40-foot (12 m) seawall to protect coastal communities, including Fudai and Otsuchi. The barrier will cost an estimated $6.8 billion.

While the tsunami of 2011 did cause damage to the floodgate in Fudai, the barrier protected the village from the main force of the waves.

An aerial view showing the damage to Otsuchi following the 2011 earthquake and tsunami. The seawall was too low to hold back the tsunami wave.

SCIENCE BIO
Michael Pritchard and LifeSaver

British inventor Michael Pritchard watched television coverage of the 2004 Indian Ocean earthquake and tsunami in horror. Knowing that there would be no clean water and survivors would have to drink contaminated water that could make them sick, he set about finding a solution. Pritchard developed a pressurized water purifier with a built-in hand pump, and his company, LifeSaver, was born. The LifeSaver purifier is portable, so it can be easily carried. It makes water from lakes, ponds, rivers, and mud puddles clean, safe, and drinkable. It can also be used to purify tap water in countries with poorly managed sewage systems. The company also created larger containers called LifeSaver Cubes with the same filtering technology that can be used at disaster sites. These were used by aid organizations during the 2018 Indonesian tsunami.

CHAPTER 4

Facing Future Disasters

Tsunamis are triggered by **geophysical** events such as earthquakes and volcanoes. These are forces that can't be stopped. But the rising ocean levels linked to climate change will have an impact on the future of tsunamis—and this is something scientists say we can have some role in changing.

Rising Sea Levels

In a 2018 study published in the scientific journal *Science Advances*, a team of scientists concluded that rising sea levels will be a game changer for tsunamis. They will make areas that are currently "tsunami safe" at risk from the massive waves. Using cutting-edge computer models, the scientists looked at how small earthquakes could cause enormous tsunamis because of the added volume of seawater. Where before, a 9.1 magnitude quake would trigger a large tsunami, in future, smaller quakes will do the same thing. The journal article noted that a 1.5-foot (0.5 m) rise in sea levels will double the risk of a massive tsunami in Macau, a coastal area in southern China. Macau is not currently an area where tsunamis are common, but it is a heavily populated area built on reclaimed lowland. The sea level there is estimated to increase 1.5 feet (0.5 m) by 2060.

The study used **COMPUTER-SIMULATED TSUNAMIS** at current sea level and with a sea-level increase of 1.5 feet (0.5 m) and 3 feet (0.9 m).

Macau is in the South China Sea region near the Manila Trench, a "megathrust" system that has lower magnitude earthquakes. It's population of 613,000 people live near the coast.

The map above shows Earth as it would appear should the Greenland and Antarctic ice sheets melt, raising ocean levels by an estimated 221 feet (67 m). More water and expanded volume enhances the risk of larger and more devastating tsunamis. Reducing our fossil fuel emissions by using alternative fuels and flying and driving less can help prevent the ice sheets from melting.

Lessening the Risk

The *Science Advances* study notes that coastal countries can build tsunami defense systems such as seawalls, but the most important factor for tsunamis in the future will be climate change mitigation. This means changing the way we live so that we use less fossil fuels. Most climate scientists believe sea levels are rising due to melting polar ice caps caused by burning fossil fuels. These fuels, including coal, oil, and gas, release carbon dioxide and other gases that trap heat in Earth's atmosphere. The world's oceans absorb most of this heat and expand when it becomes warmer. This is called thermal expansion.

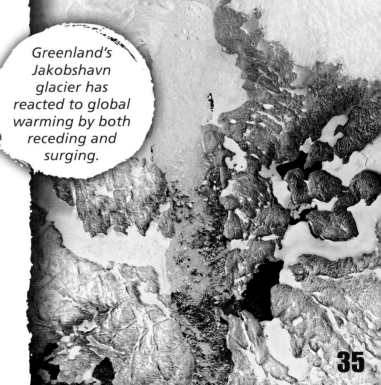

Greenland's Jakobshavn glacier has reacted to global warming by both receding and surging.

Other Human Activity

While human activity doesn't cause tsunamis, it can make the effects of them worse. Natural shoreline protections, including **mangroves** and coral reefs, act as shock absorbers for the onrushing waters of a tsunami. The problem is that humans have destroyed these in recent years.

Mangroves

Mangroves are the only types of trees and shrubs than can tolerate salt water. They grow close to rivers, estuaries, and the sea in the world's tropical regions. Mangroves play an important part in protecting coastlines from tsunamis. Mangrove forests soak up destructive wave energy and help to stop **coastal erosion**. After the 2004 tsunami in Aceh, Indonesia, that country began replanting mangrove forests on the coast to restore ecologically damaged coastlines. Some scientific studies have shown villages located behind mangrove forests had 8 percent fewer deaths after the tsunami.

Mangroves' dense roots slow down water flow and reduce erosion.

Planting wide areas of mangroves can help lessen tsunami damage because waves are reduced as they pass through the trees.

Coral Reefs

Coral reefs are also important in reducing the impact of tsunamis. The reefs are natural **breakwaters**. They provide a barrier that reduces the force of a wave before it reaches the shore. When a tsunami arrives, it hits coral reefs at first. This slows down the waves. These waves are then slowed down further by the mangroves. Even if the waves keep going, they will not be moving as fast. There will therefore be less damage from the tsunami. The reefs are also damaged during tsunamis, when debris rips them up and tosses them ashore. Some are broken or covered in sediment and take years to recover.

Coastal Features

In many populated areas, natural features along coasts have been removed or altered as towns and cities have grown. There has also been an increase in the number of industrial operations such as shrimp farms in these areas. Areas with larger populations mean greater loss of life when a disaster occurs. Some coastal mangrove forests have been destroyed or altered by the building of massive tourist hotels and resorts. These human alterations have made shorelines more at risk from tsunamis.

Australia's Great Barrier Reef is the largest coral reef system in the world. Climate change and coastal development are both threats to the reef.

Satellite Information

Satellites can give scientists a better understanding of ocean circulation and the effect of this on the world's climate. They can also help create accurate maps, monitor tides, and assess the effects climate change has on sea levels. The Jason and TOPEX/Poseidon satellites collected very important data during the 2004 Indian Ocean tsunami.

Studying Data

The TOPEX/Poseidon satellite was launched in 1992 as a joint project between **NASA** and CNES, the French space agency.

Its mission ended in 2006, but not before it provided data that has helped scientists understand how tsunamis effect coastline features. The Jason-1 satellite was launched in 2001. It provided data from orbit until 2012. Jason-3 is the latest version of the satellite.

Jason-3 also studies ocean circulation and currents, rising sea levels, the ocean's heat content, and the effects of climate change. Data from the satellite is used to study how tsunamis work. Studying weather patterns also helps scientists to predict climate change. The information these satellites provide can be used to produce computer models of future tsunamis and answer important questions about how their effects can be lessened.

*Satellites in orbit can detect increases in radio and **infrared** radiation before an earthquake. Improvements in technology could mean that radiation, and tsunamis, are detected earlier.*

People can find satellite information from Jason-3 on NASA's Physical Oceanography Distributed Active Archive Center (PO.DAAC) website.

Understanding Tsunamis

Satellite data from Jason-3 is stored at NASA's Physical Oceanography Distributed Active Archive Center (PO.DAAC) in Pasadena, California. This organization makes ocean and climate data gathered by NASA available to everyone. Scientists from all over the world can use and study the information gathered by Jason-3. This helps them to better understand tsunamis and test different theories on how to lessen their impact, or make communities more resilient to them.

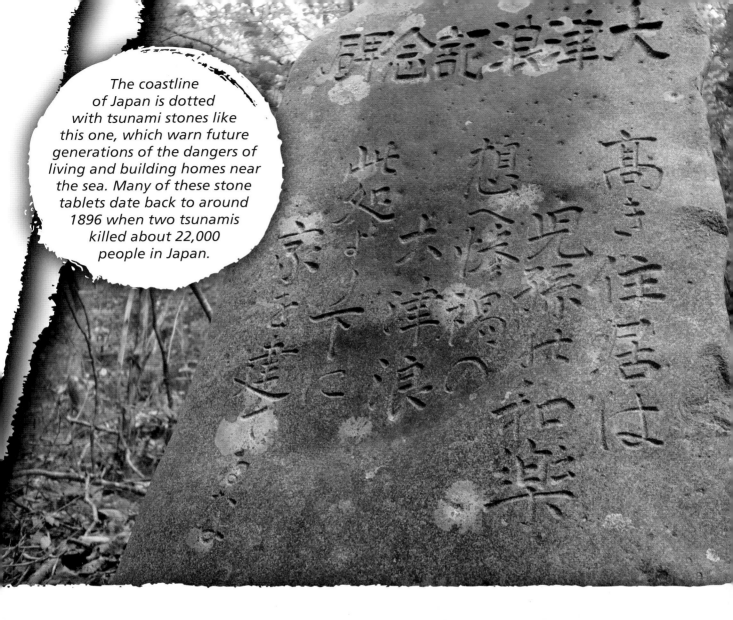

The coastline of Japan is dotted with tsunami stones like this one, which warn future generations of the dangers of living and building homes near the sea. Many of these stone tablets date back to around 1896 when two tsunamis killed about 22,000 people in Japan.

Luck and Resilience

For hundreds of years, people in Japan described communities that survived tsunamis with little damage as "lucky." Regions that were destroyed were considered "unlucky." Experience and scientific research has shown that tsunami survival is more than just luck. Geography, infrastructure, and the wealth of areas affected by tsunamis has a lot to do with tsunami resilience, or the ability to withstand the tsunami and also recover quickly from its effects.

Vulnerability

Research shows that communities that are more vulnerable to tsunamis have little protection from them. Protection includes natural barriers such as mangrove forests, coastal sand dunes, and hills above a community, and human-made barriers such as well-constructed seawalls. It also includes building codes requiring that new buildings be constructed with earthquake- and tsunami-resistant materials.

Higher Ground

In the 2011 Great East Japan earthquake and tsunami, the village of Yoshihama survived 59-foot (18 m) waves with just one death and 11 houses lost. The village had experienced tsunamis in 1896, with 204 deaths and 36 houses lost, and in 1933, with 17 deaths and 15 houses washed away. After that, the village moved houses higher up, away from the coast. Not many communities can relocate because it costs too much. But in wealthier areas of the world, governments can map areas where tsunami waves are likely to hit and prevent new homes from being built there.

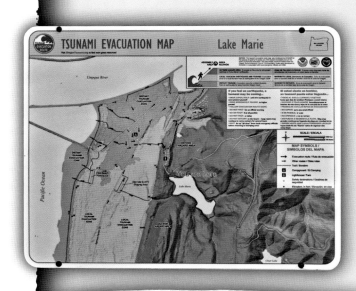

The state of Oregon is changing its land-use plan to include tsunami resilience measures. These include directions on how to locate hospitals, schools, and police stations out of tsunami areas.

SCIENCE BIO
Dr. Lori Dengler, Guiding Preparedness

In her 2015 children's book *The Extraordinary Voyage of Kamome: A Tsunami Boat Comes Home*, Lori Dengler and Amya Miller tell of a Japanese fishing boat that was swept away by a March 2011 tsunami in Japan. After two years at sea, the boat found its way to Crescent City, California, and became the focus of a U.S.-Japan outreach program. Dr. Dengler used the book to teach children about tsunamis, disasters, and resilience.

A geology professor at Humboldt State University in California, Dengler is an expert on tsunamis and hazard mitigation.

Her work has been credited with preparing coastal communities for tsunamis in California and around the world. She co-authored a United Nations post-tsunami field guide that helps aid workers understand their mission and work in countries hit by tsunamis.

Dr. Dengler has also taken part in post-tsunami survey teams in Papua New Guinea, Peru, and Indonesia, and has served on a national tsunami mitigation committee. She was awarded a National Oceanic and Atmospheric Administration (NOAA) award for her tsunami work.

CHAPTER 5

Building on the Past

We can't prevent tsunamis, but there are many things we can do to limit the effects they have on humans and human societies. One thing we can do is learn from the past and develop and use new technologies and new ways of living.

By studying previous tsunamis, researchers determine what factors led to the loss of life and destruction of property. Using this information helps experts determine where to locate new development, how buildings should be constructed to withstand natural hazards, and how we can help people recover from disasters and rebuild their lives and communities.

Some countries are at the forefront of tsunami resilience. They can afford to invest in expensive alert systems, such as Japan's network of seismic pressure sensors on the ocean floor. These provide more accurate information on earthquakes that generate tsunamis—and more timely warnings—thereby improving tsunami resilience. Other countries don't have the money to protect their citizens with high-tech systems. They must stick with the rule of heading to high ground after feeling the strong shakes of a quake. With rising sea levels making tsunamis more of a threat, it is important that the rest of the world do its part in trying to stop climate change.

TSUNAMI HAZARD ZONE

IN CASE OF EARTHQUAKE, GO TO HIGH GROUND OR INLAND

What to do in case of a
Tsunami Alert

When there is an Tsunami Alert, an alarm will sound throughout the resort. Hotel Ambassadors who are part of the Emergency Response Team (ERT) will be deployed around the property, and begin to usher guest to safety.

1. During such an alert, please give your full co-operation to ERT Ambassadors.
2. Instructions will be given to all guests to make their way to the Lobby on Level 4.
3. Personal belongings, unless within personal reach, should be left behind, as your personal safety is our priority.
4. Use stairs only to ascend to the Lobby. Elevators are not to be used.
5. Do Not Run. Walk in a brisk but calm fashion.
6. Do not panic in any way that may cause others to react the same, as this will hinder the efforts of our ERT.
7. If you are concerned about a member of your family or group, please inform an ERT Ambassador, giving a description and the last known location of this person.
8. On reaching the Lobby await further instruction from ERT Ambassadors.
9. Do not, for any reason, leave this area until instructed to do so.

Relief workers load supplies onto a helicopter for delivery to Sri Lanka following the Indian Ocean earthquake and tsunami in 2004.

Ask Yourself This

Based on the information in this book, what are some of the ways in which humans have learned from devastating tsunamis and their aftereffects over the years?

1. Tsunamis are a natural event, but what kinds of human activities might add to their destructive power?

2. What kinds of new technologies are being developed to study tsunamis and lessen the impact disasters have on people?

3. Imagine that you're living in a part of the world that is prone to tsunamis. What kinds of things can you do to lessen the impact of a tsunami, while it's happening and during its aftermath?

Bibliography

Chapter 1

"Information on tsunamis." Natural Resources Canada, March 11, 2019. https://bit.ly/2yYpE2t

"Krakatoa." *Encyclopedia Britannica*, May 2, 2019. https://bit.ly/2zqGPYu

Lee, Jane J. "The 2011 Japan Tsunami Was Caused By Largest Fault Slip Ever Recorded." *National Geographic*, December 7, 2013. https://bit.ly/2J8M5qb

Lehnardt, Karin. "50 Interesting Tsunami Facts." Fact Retriever, August 12, 2019. https://bit.ly/2CHnoN4

"Mar 11, 2011 CE: Tohoku Earthquake and Tsunami." *National Geographic*, December 27, 2004. https://bit.ly/2GfEHZT

"May 22, 1960 CE: Valdivia Earthquake Strikes Chile." *National Geographic*. https://bit.ly/2CNd9aG

Meixler, Eli. "As Indonesia Reels from the Earthquake and Tsunami, Experts Warn of More Deadly Disasters to Come." *Time*, October 11, 2018. https://bit.ly/2FTxX3I

"Messina earthquake and tsunami of 1908." *Encyclopaedia Britannica*, December 21, 2018. https://bit.ly/2Ll6PZK

"Minoan eruption." New World Encyclopedia, May 30, 2019. https://bit.ly/2HqIzWT

"Once and Future Tsunamis." *PBS*, March 2005. https://to.pbs.org/343ytE8

Oskin, Becky. "Japan Earthquake & Tsunami of 2011: Facts and Information." LiveScience, September 13, 2017. https://bit.ly/2h22I9R

Pallardy, Richard. "Chile earthquake of 1960." *Encyclopaedia Britannica*, May 15, 2019. https://bit.ly/2cNoit6

Phillips, Campbell. "The 10 most destructive tsunamis in history." *Australian Geographic*, March 16, 2011. https://bit.ly/2PUMUGb

Rafferty, John P., and Kenneth Pletcher. "Japan earthquake and tsunami of 2011." *Encyclopaedia Britannica*, March 4, 2019. https://bit.ly/2gDE4vp

Reid, Kathryn. "2011 Japan earthquake and tsunami: Facts, FAQs, and how to help." World Vision, May 7, 2018. https://bit.ly/2L7SuiH

Rinkesh. "Tsunami Facts." Conserve Energy Future. https://bit.ly/2L5LxQs

"Tsunami and Earthquake Research." U.S. Geological Survey. https://on.doi.gov/2zriNwc

"Tsunami Facts." Cool Kid Facts. www.coolkidfacts.com/tsunami-facts-for-kids

"Tsunamis." Department of Homeland Security. www.ready.gov/tsunamis

"Tsunamis." *National Geographic*. https://on.natgeo.com/2zRt0Au

Whipps, Heather. "How the Eruption of Thera Changed the World." LiveScience, February 25, 2008. https://bit.ly/2rdKaq2

Chapter 2

"2004 Indian Ocean earthquake." New World Encyclopedia. https://bit.ly/2U85j20 "Tsunamis." *National Geographic*. https://on.natgeo.com/2zRt0Au

Bolt, Bruce A. "Earthquake." *Encyclopaedia Britannica*, August 7, 2019. https://bit.ly/2tNyPxf

Bolt, Bruce A. "Volcanism." *Encyclopaedia Britannica*, August 7, 2019. https://bit.ly/2F7TgLM

"Earthquake." *Science Daily*. https://bit.ly/2xvd1JB

"Information on tsunamis." Natural Resources Canada, November 19, 2018. https://bit.ly/2yYpE2t

Lehnardt, Karin. "50 Interesting Tsunami Facts." Fact Retriever, August 12, 2019. www.factretriever.com/tsunami-facts

Lotha, Gloria. "Indian Ocean tsunami of 2004." *Encyclopaedia Britannica*, March 13, 2019. https://bit.ly/2gyuBUo

Rinkesh. "Tsunami Facts." Conserve Energy Future. https://bit.ly/2L5LxQs

Rodgers, Lucy, and Gerry Fletcher. "Indian Ocean tsunami: Then and now." *BBC News*, December 25, 2014. https://bbc.in/2Bym26C

"The Deadliest Tsunami in History?" *National Geographic*, December 27, 2004. https://bit.ly/2ZiRSSU

"Tsunami." *Encyclopaedia Britannica*, August 1, 2019. www.britannica.com/science/tsunami

"Tsunami and Earthquake Research." U.S. Geological Survey. https://on.doi.gov/2zriNwc

"Tsunami Facts." Cool Kid Facts. https://bit.ly/2HsL0r2

"Tsunami Fast Facts." *CNN*, March 5, 2019. https://cnn.it/2Lc4Ac3

"Tsunamis." Department of Homeland Security. www.ready.gov/tsunamis

"What causes an earthquake?" Australian Academy of Science. https://bit.ly/2XFW4qJ

"What causes earthquakes?" British Geological Survey. https://bit.ly/2KL2fq7

"Why and where do earthquakes occur?" British Geological Survey. https://bit.ly/2WCsilj

Chapter 3

"Bill McGuire." *The Guardian*. www.theguardian.com/profile/billmcguire

"Deep Ocean Tsunami Detection Buoys." Australian Government Bureau of Meteorology. https://bit.ly/2BLaIlr

Griffiths, James. "How Indonesia's tsunami warning system failed its citizens again." *CNN*, December 24, 2018. https://cnn.it/2QNDBJx

Hastwell, Annie, and Genelle Weule. "What is a tsunami and how are they monitored?" June 20, 2017. https://ab.co/2EXeM5R

"Indonesia earthquake and tsunami: How warning system failed the victims." *BBC News*, October 1, 2018. https://bbc.in/2DMWlmu

"Japan Is Building a 40-foot Wall to Stop Tsunamis." Smithsonian.com, March 27, 2015. https://bit.ly/2LfFidd

Knight, Will. "How Japan's Earthquake and Tsunami Warning Systems Work." *MIT Technology Review*, March 11, 2011. https://bit.ly/2kdXyJ9

Lehnardt, Karin. "50 Interesting Tsunami Facts." Fact Retriever, August 12, 2019. www.factretriever.com/tsunami-facts

NOAA Center for Tsunami Research https://nctr.pmel.noaa.gov

O'Brien, Miles, and Marsha Walton. "Making Waves, Saving Lives." Science Nation, December 14, 2009. https://bit.ly/2zkR5kX

"Prof Bill McGuire." UCL Earth Sciences. https://bit.ly/2NCmmIb

"Tsunami warning systems: Lessons from Japan." *VOA News*, March 14, 2011. https://bit.ly/2KWFMG4

"What is a tsunami?" National Oceanic and Atmospheric Administration, September 29, 2017. https://bit.ly/2G4ue14

Chapter 4

Bond, Michael. "Tsunami defences-can you keep the waves at bay?" Engineering and Technology, April 15, 2011. http://bit.ly/2zsLSr2

Corkill, Edan. "Heights of survival." *The Japan Times*. http://bit.ly/2HsQv9k

"DART (Deep-ocean Assessment and Reporting of Tsunamis)." NOAA Center for Tsunami Research. https://nctr.pmel.noaa.gov/Dart

"Deep-ocean Assessment and Reporting of Tsunamis (DART)." NOAA Center for Tsunami Research. http://bit.ly/2MEwAIv

"Deep Ocean Detection Buoys." Australian Government Bureau of Meteorology. http://bit.ly/2PhWTGJ

"Dr. Walter Dudley Projects." Pacific Tsunami Museum. http://tsunami.org/dr-walter-dudley-projects/

"Earthquake Relief." American Red Cross. https://rdcrss.org/2KJJKIS

"Earthquake rescue: How survivors are found." *BBC News*. https://bbc.in/2ZmcJQM

Grinthal, Dan. "Responding to Natural Disasters." *Reporter Magazine*, April 23, 2018. http://bit.ly/31sKeCH

Hannaford, Kat. "This Unwanted Monstrosity of a Floodgate Saved a Japanese Village from Tsunami Ruin." Gizmodo, May 13, 2011. http://bit.ly/30CuL21

Hardy, Michael. "Ominous Views of Japan's New Concrete Seawalls." *Wired*, April 26, 2018. http://bit.ly/32apjnl

Hosaka, Tomoko A.. "Once-belittled floodgate saved Japanese town." *The Spokesman-Review*, May 15, 2011. http://bit.ly/2Zry4HX

"Indian Tsunami Early Warning System." ESSO-Indian National Centre for Ocean Information Services. https://bit.ly/2IJ3OdG

"Indian Ocean tsunami warning system." *BBC News*, December 23, 2005. https://bbc.in/2ZsZwoP

Jacobs, Sarah."'It feels like we're in jail': Japan spent $12 billion on seawalls after the devastating 2011 tsunami—and now locals are feeling like prisoners." *Business Insider*, March 12, 2018. http://bit.ly/2KZDNRp

Knight, Will. "How Japan's Earthquake and Tsunami Warning Systems Work." *MIT Technology Review*, March 11, 2011. http://bit.ly/2L4R9dO

Kyung-hoon, Kim. "After the tsunami: Japan's sea walls in pictures." *The Guardian*, March 9, 2018. http://bit.ly/2MNk9KL

Lamb, Kate, and Luke Harding. "Indonesia earthquake: lack of equipment hampers rescue efforts." *The Guardian*, August 6, 2018. http://bit.ly/2I9ue0N

"Nepal earthquake: How does the search and rescue operation work?" *BBC News*, April 27, 2015. https://bbc.in/31sCSPH

NOAA Center for Tsunami Research https://nctr.pmel.noaa.gov

Rupli, Robin. "Transcript: Interview with American Tsunami Expert Walter Dudley." *VOA News*, October 30, 2009. http://bit.ly/2KX7Nxc

Salgado, Julia. "Types of Seawalls." Sciencing, April 25, 2017. http://bit.ly/2U8F9ft

"Search and rescue response and coordination (natural disasters)." UNHCR. http://bit.ly/2F5L12W

"Sulawesi Quake and Tsunami: Red Cross Aid and New Devastation." American Red Cross, October 4, 2018. https://rdcrss.org/2LeP7YZ

"The Fundamentals of Emergency Response." Direct Relief. http://bit.ly/2XF2tm4

"The Indian Tsunami Early Warning System (ITEWS)." The United Nations. https://bit.ly/2Htj71Q

"Tsunami." *Encyclopaedia Britannica*, August 1, 2019. www.britannica.com/science/tsunami

"Tsunami Facts and Information." Australian Government Bureau of Meteorology. http://bit.ly/2UcXcBw

"Tsunami Message Definitions." NOAA/National Weather Service. http://bit.ly/2zpzsAl

"Tsunami Warning Systems: Lessons from Japan." *VOA News*, March 14, 2011. http://bit.ly/320PDQS

"Understanding the Difference Between a Tsunami 'Watch' and 'Warning.' University of Hawaii, at Hilo. http://bit.ly/2U9OrrD

"Walter Dudley." University of Washington. http://bit.ly/2HurTwE

"What is a tsunami?" National Oceanic and Atmospheric Administration, September 29, 2017. http://bit.ly/2MFOPgG

Chapter 5

"Ecological Consequences of Natural Disasters: Tsunami." World Wildlife Fund. http://bit.ly/2Zt5Pgh

Garthwaite-Stanford, Josie. "New Tsunami Warnings Could Get More People to Safety." *Futurity*, January 22, 2019. http://bit.ly/2PihXN9

"How does Australia's tsunami warning system work?" Australian Government, Bureau of Meteorology, September 8, 2016. http://bit.ly/2NAFGpy

Hudson, Andrew. "New technology aims to track earthquakes and tsunamis in real-time." *Haida Gwaii Observer*, April 13, 2018. http://bit.ly/2FhDNJt

"Human activities contributed to tsunami's ravages: environmental expert." *Terra Daily*, December 27, 2004. http://bit.ly/2zqkPN8

"Jason-3." National Environmental Satellite Data and information Service. http://bit.ly/30JNUPW

"Jason-3 Oceanographic Mission Satellite." Aerospace Technology. http://bit.ly/342BkNx

Kadri, Usama, and Chiang C. Mei. "New Real-Time Tsunami Early Warning System Calculates Size and Distance Using Underwater Sound Waves." *Scientific American*, January 24, 2018. http://bit.ly/30DV3B8

Lehnardt, Karin. "50 Interesting Tsunami Facts." Fact Retriever, August 12, 2019. www.factretriever.com/tsunami-facts

"Lori Dengler." Humboldt State University. http://bit.ly/2KZG1QL

"Missions: Jason-3." NASA Jet Propulsion Laboratory. https://go.nasa.gov/2zqlk9Y

"NASA Monitoring Technologies Shake Up Earthquake Prediction." *Tech Briefs*, April 1, 2016. http://bit.ly/2XDYAO9

"NASA Tsunami Research Makes Waves in the Scientific Community." NASA, January 17, 2008. https://go.nasa.gov/342qoPT

"Natural disasters made worse by human activity." Expatica, May 20, 2008. http://bit.ly/2LgCtIG

Nimura, Tamiko. "Books: Kamome: A Tsunami Boat Comes Home." *Hyphen*, Asian America Unabridged, June 2, 2016. http://bit.ly/2Udo7Np

PO.DAAC. https://podaac.jpl.nasa.gov/AboutPodaac

"TOPEX/Poseidon." NASA Jet Propulsion Laboratory. https://sealevel.jpl.nasa.gov/missions/topex

"TOPEX/Poseidon Satellites." NASA Ocean Motion, January 5, 2006. http://bit.ly/2KZ1KIy

45

Learning More

Books

Swanson, Jennifer. *Tsunamis.* Core Library, 2013.

Larson, Kirsten. *Tsunamis.* Rourke Educational Media, 2015.

Winchester, Simon. *When the Earth Shakes: Earthquakes, Volcanoes, and Tsunamis.* Viking Books for Young Readers, 2015.

Websites

Learn more about tsunamis.
www.britannica.com/science/tsunami

Read all about the ten most destructive tsunamis in history.
https://bit.ly/2wN5A1l

Learn all about tsunami research and forecasting.
https://nctr.pmel.noaa.gov

Read about the 2011 tsunami and nuclear accident in Japan.
www.britannica.com/event/Japan-earthquake-and-tsunami-of-2011

Glossary

adapt To change behavior so that it is easier to live in a particular place or situation

Atlantis A legendary kingdom that is supposed to have sunk beneath the sea thousands of years ago

breakwaters Barriers that break the force of waves, such as in a harbor

buoys Floats in the water that mark a channel or a hazard

carbon dioxide A gas produced by people and animals breathing out or by some chemical reactions

cholera A disease caused by bacteria in drinking water

climate change Changing weather patterns over time generally considered to be caused by human activity such as fossil fuel use

coastal erosion The process by which the land on the coast is worn away by the action of water, glaciers, wind, or waves

composition What something is made up of

contaminated When something is made impure by the addition of something harmful

current A body of water moving in a certain direction

debris Pieces of something that has been destroyed

displaced When something is moved out of its original location

Doctors Without Borders An international organization of medical professionals

dysentery An intestinal infection causing severe diarrhea

earthquakes Sudden and violent shaking of the ground caused by movements within Earth's crust or volcanic action

electromagnetic The electrical and magnetic forces produced by an electrical current

evacuation To send people to a place of safety

geophysical Relating to the study of Earth's physical movements and forces

infrared Radiation similar to light but with a longer wavelength, so we need special equipment to see it

infrastructure Things such as transportation, buildings, communications, and power supplies that a society needs to function

landslides A large amount of earth and rocks falling down a mountain or cliff

magnitude The size of an earthquake

mangroves Trees or shrubs that grow in tropical coastal swamps that are flooded at high tide

meteors Small bodies of matter from outer space that enter Earth's atmosphere

Minoan civilization A civilization that lived on the island of Crete from 3000 to 1450 B.C.E.

NASA The National Aeronautics and Space Administration, a United States government organization focused on spacecraft and space exploration

nuclear plant A facility that converts atomic energy into power

radar A system for detecting objects by sending out pulses of high-frequency electromagnetic waves that are reflected off the object back to the source

radiation Energy that comes from a nuclear reaction

Red Cross An international organization that helps people during times of war and natural disaster

satellites Artificial bodies placed in orbit to collect information or for communications

seismic Relating to earthquakes or other vibrations of Earth and its crust

sensors Devices that sense or detect something, then react to it in a certain way

simulated Created processes to look or act like something real

sirens Devices that provide signals or warnings with a loud prolonged sound

sonar A system that detects objects under water and for measuring the water's depth. The device sends out sound pulses and measures their return after being reflected.

thermal imaging Using equipment to detect the heat produced by people or other things to create images

United Nations An organization made up of 193 countries that works to promote peace and human rights around the world

volcanic eruptions The sudden and violent discharge of steam and volcanic material from a volcano

Index

About the Author

Simon Rose is the author of 15 novels and more than 100 nonfiction books for children and young adults. He is also a writing instructor who offers online workshops and courses for children and adults.